Oxford First Encyclopedia
Animals and Plants

Andrew Langley

OXFORD

OXFORD
UNIVERSITY PRESS

Great Clarendon Street, Oxford OX2 6DP

Oxford University Press is a department of the University of Oxford.
It furthers the University's objective of excellence in research, scholarship,
and education by publishing worldwide in

Oxford New York

Auckland Bangkok Buenos Aires Cape Town Chennai
Dar es Salaam Delhi Hong Kong Istanbul Karachi Kolkata
Kuala Lumpur Madrid Melbourne Mexico City Mumbai Nairobi
São Paulo Shanghai Singapore Taipei Tokyo Toronto

with an associated company in Berlin

Oxford is a registered trade mark of Oxford University Press
in the UK and in certain other countries

© Andrew Langley 1999, 2002

The moral rights of the author have been asserted

Database right Oxford University Press (maker)

First published in 1999
Second edition 2002

British Library Cataloguing in Publication Data available

ISBN 0-19-910971-0

10 9 8 7 6 5 4 3

Printed in Malaysia

Contents

Animals and Plants

People are not the only living things on the Earth. We share it with many millions of other animals and plants. They live in every part of the world, from the bottom of the deepest ocean to the top of the highest mountain. Some plants and animals are huge. Others are so tiny that you need a microscope to see them.

The lives of animals and plants join together in a complicated way that we call "the balance of nature". A snail eats a leaf. A bird eats the snail. A fox eats the bird. Each one depends on the other for food.

How plants grow

Wherever you live, you will find plants. Some are grown specially by farmers to give us food, timber and other useful materials. But most plants are wild. There are thousands of different kinds of wild plants, growing in many different places: hot, dry deserts, damp forests, under ice and snow – even in cities!

Parts of a plant

Plants that produce flowers are called "flowering plants". Each part of the plant has an important job to do. The roots take up water, and hold the plant firmly in the ground. The stem supports the leaves, flowers and fruit. The leaves make the plant's food, and the flowers make fruits and seeds. One day, the seeds will start to grow into new plants.

▷ Plants can make their own food. All they need is air, water and sunlight. They use sunlight to turn water and a gas called carbon dioxide from the air into a sugary food called sap. This happens inside the leaves. The sap travels through the plant's stems, from the leaves to wherever the plant needs food.

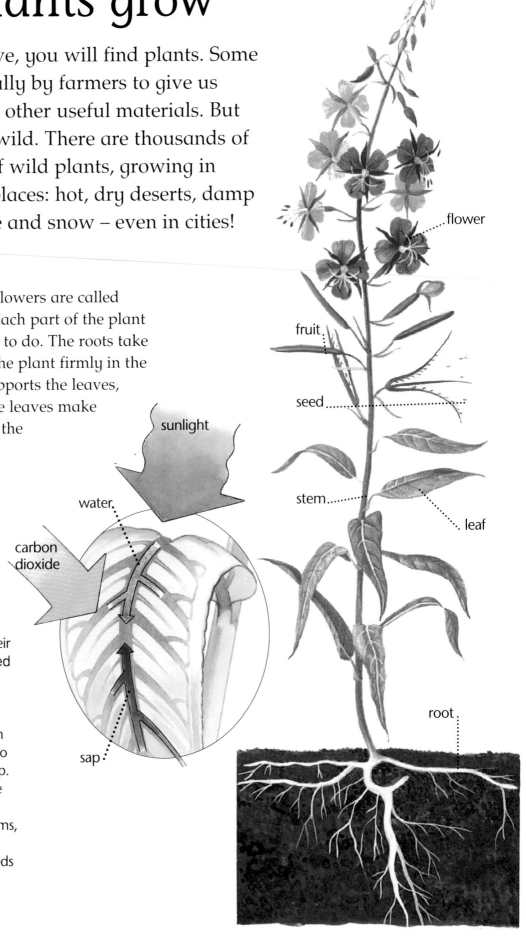

flower

fruit

seed

sunlight

water

carbon dioxide

stem

leaf

sap

root

Flowers and seeds

The reason plants have flowers is to help pass tiny grains called pollen from one plant to another. The plants need this pollen to make seeds. In some flowers, the pollen is blown from place to place by the wind. Other flowers get insects to carry their pollen for them. With the help of the pollen, the flower can make seeds.

◁ The sweet smell and bright colour of many flowers attract insects. The insects come to collect delicious nectar from inside the flower. As the insect drinks the nectar, tiny grains of pollen stick to its body. When the insect visits another flower, it leaves some pollen behind.

All kinds of plants

Not all plants have flowers. Plants come in all shapes and sizes, from tiny mosses to huge trees. Here are some of the many other kinds of plant.

▽ A moss is a very simple kind of plant. It has no flowers. It makes tiny, dust-like spores instead of seeds.

◁ A mushroom is a kind of fungus. It never has flowers. It gets its food from dead plant material in the soil.

▷ Trees like this Scots pine have a tall, straight trunk and thin leaves like needles. They make their seeds inside woody cones.

Grow plants from seeds

It is easy to grow your own plants. All you need is a saucer, some kitchen paper towels and a packet of seeds (mustard and cress seeds are the easiest). Soak the paper towels in water and put them on the saucer. Then sprinkle the seeds on top, and put the saucer on a sunny window-sill. Make sure the towels stay damp. Your seeds will soon start to sprout.

Animal families

Mammals are the only animals with fur or hair on their bodies. All mammals drink milk from their mothers when they are young. Bats, whales and monkeys are mammals – and so are you!

Birds are the only animals with feathers. They are born from eggs with hard shells. Birds have strong wings in the same place that you have arms. Not all birds can fly. Ostriches can only walk or run, while penguins use their wings for swimming.

Most **reptiles** live on dry land. Their skin is covered with tough, dry scales. We say that reptiles are "cold-blooded" because the temperature of their body depends on their surroundings. Lizards, snakes, crocodiles and turtles are all reptiles.

Amphibians are born in the water, but when they are grown up they can live on land. Like reptiles, they are cold-blooded animals. Frogs, toads and newts are all amphibians.

Fish live in water. Their bodies are covered in scales, and they have fins to help them swim. Fish can breathe underwater. They have special parts called gills which take oxygen from the water.

Animals come in lots of shapes and sizes. Some are furry and some are scaly. Some have hard shells and some have feathers. Some animals are enormous, like the blue whale, and some are tiny, like the flea. Scientists think that altogether, there are more than 10 million different kinds, or species, of animal!

Animal groups

Scientists have made it easier for us to tell one animal from another. They have arranged animals that are similar to each other into groups, in the same way that books about the same subject are put together on a library shelf. Above are some of the main animal groups.

Worms and more worms

There are more roundworms than any other kind of animal. These tiny worms live in the sea and on land. Scientists believe that there are at least 40,000,000,000,000,000,000,000,000 of them!

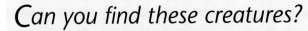

Can you find these creatures?

butterfly	ostrich
catfish	rat
crab	shark
crocodile	snail
elephant	snake
frog	spider
millipede	surgeon fish (a kind
newt	of flatfish)
octopus	swallow

Arthropods do not have bones inside them. Instead, they have a hard skin or shell that covers the outside of their body. Arthropods have at least three pairs of legs. Insects are the most common arthropods, and there are 8 million different kinds of insect!

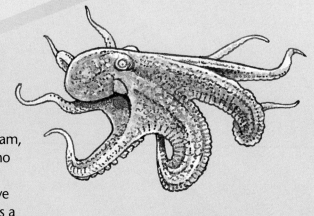

Molluscs have a soft body, with a hard shell around it. Some, like the clam, have two shells. Molluscs have no legs, but many have a kind of "foot" to help them move about. An octopus is a mollusc with its shell inside its body.

Prehistoric life

Long ago, there were no people on the Earth. There were no animals at all. Very slowly, over millions of years, the first living things developed. They were made of just one tiny cell. These living things gradually changed and grew bigger. They became plants and animals, and lived in the sea. Some animals grew legs and began to live on land. Many different kinds of animals developed. Soon they filled every part of the Earth.

The beginning of life

Among the first creatures were simple water plants called algae. Later plants began to grow on land. Giant ferns and horsetails covered much of the world. The first animals were tiny sea creatures, with tails for swimming. Then animals became bigger, and grew bony skeletons. The first land animals were amphibians, which were followed by reptiles (including dinosaurs). Mammals and birds were the last kinds of animals to appear.

3000

single-cell animals

2000

algae

1000

jellyfish

trilobites

giant ferns

first fish with jaws

500

first amphibians

400

first reptiles

first dinosaurs

first mammals

flying insects

300

200

first birds

first apes

first humans

100

present day

Age of the dinosaurs

Dinosaurs were the most successful kind of early animal. The word dinosaur means "terrible lizard". Some dinosaurs were enormous. *Brachiosaurus* was as big as five elephants! Some, such as *Tyrannosaurus rex*, were very fierce. Other dinosaurs were only the size of a cat or dog. The age of the dinosaurs lasted for a long time, but the last ones died out millions of years ago.

▷ How do we know what dinosaurs looked like? After all, they died long before the first people lived on Earth. But the dinosaurs did not completely disappear. The skeletons of some of them turned into rock. These rocky remains are called "fossils".

▷ Pterosaurs had wings to help them fly or glide.

▽ The stegosaur had bony plates along its back.

▽ *Parasaurolophus* was a plant-eater. Its long, hollow crest may have acted as a trumpet.

▽ The plesiosaur lived in the sea and ate fish.

◁ *Tyrannosaurus rex* had huge sharp teeth. It hunted other animals and ate them.

! Dinosaurs are alive!

Dinosaurs may be dead, but some closely related animals are still alive. Crocodiles, lizards and snakes are all part of the dinosaur family. And birds may really be flying dinosaurs!

▷ *Deinonychus* was a frightening hunter. Its name means "terrible claw".

Wildlife in a meadow

When you lie down in a grass meadow, you are in the middle of a miniature world. It looks like a jungle, with a tangle of grass stems, leaves and roots. All around you insects are busy searching for food. Crickets munch on young grass. Tiger beetles hunt for ants. Up above, bumble bees collect sugary nectar from the flowers. Field mice, rabbits and birds are here too – they seem like giants!

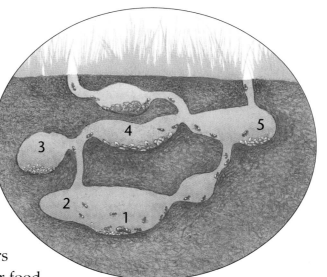

An ants' nest

A huge number of ants live inside an ants' nest. But it is started by just one ant – the queen. The queen ant lays her eggs under the ground. They hatch and become ant grubs, which grow into worker ants. The workers build the nest and gather food, while the queen goes on and on laying eggs. In the end, the nest may contain over 100,000 ants!

1 queen ant
2 worker ants
3 eggs
4 grubs
5 food

Fast food

Rabbits love to nibble grass and other green plants. But grass is tough food. It takes a long time to break down, or digest. So the rabbit eats it twice! First, the chewed grass passes out of the rabbit's body as little pellets. Then the rabbit eats the pellets. This way, it gets twice as much goodness from the grass.

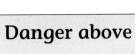

Danger above

High above the meadow flies the kestrel. This bird is a meat-eater. It hunts for small animals such as voles or mice. The kestrel can hover in the air and stay in one place, even in a strong wind. When it spots a mouse, it swoops down very quickly and grabs the animal with its strong feet.

Moles

The mole digs long tunnels under the ground. It pushes the earth up to the surface, making mounds that we call molehills. These tunnels are not just a home for the mole - they are traps, too. Earthworms fall down into them and provide an easy meal. Sometimes there are so many worms that the mole stores them for later.

! Frantic Fliers

Some insects have to work very hard to fly. A butterfly beats its wings about 10 times each second. The tiny midge beats its wings 1,000 times a second!

Wildlife on the grasslands

The grassland, or savannah, of East Africa looks bare and dry, but it is full of food. Plant-eating animals like giraffes and elephants chew the leaves or twigs of trees. Herds of zebra and gazelle feed on the grass. But there are also meat-eaters here. Lions and cheetahs hunt the zebras and gazelles. Any meat they leave is quickly finished up by jackals and vultures.

△ Giraffes are the tallest animals in the world. They use their long necks to feed from the highest branches of trees, where other animals cannot reach.

wildebee

locust

secretary bird

Grass: the wonder plant

Savannah grass sometimes grows as tall as 3 metres. It provides food for many animals, big and small. Zebras eat the top part of the grass. Wildebeeste eat the leafy centre. Gazelles eat the short, young shoots. Birds eat the grass seeds. Beetles munch the dead leaves.

oxpecker

gazelle

lion

zebra

△ Big brown mounds stick up out of the flat land. They are twice as tall as a person! Yet these mounds are built by millions of tiny termites, as a city to live in. The mounds are so strong that few animals can damage them.

△ Would you like an oxpecker on your back? Its sharp claws would dig into you as you walked along. But zebras do not mind giving this bird a lift. This is because the oxpeckers eat up the tiny, itchy insects called ticks which burrow under the zebras' skins.

Speedy cheetahs

The cheetah is the fastest of all land animals. With its long legs and slim body, it is built for speed. It can run at more than 80 kilometres an hour, for short bursts. At that speed, it can easily catch a gazelle or an antelope.

Wildlife in a woodland

This forest is in northern USA. Most of the trees here have broad, flat leaves, so they are called broad-leaf trees! They are home for many different birds and insects. Larger animals shelter or hide in the shade beneath the trees. In summer, the millions of leaves block out most of the sunlight. But in autumn the leaves fall, and the forest becomes more light and open.

▷ A broadleaf tree makes a perfect snack bar for many kinds of bird. Warblers and blue jays hunt for insects and caterpillars. The sapsucker drills holes in the tree with its beak, then drinks the juicy sap. The acorn woodpecker drills holes, too. It uses them to store acorns and berries for the winter.

Falling leaves

In autumn the weather gets colder. The leaves of the broadleaf trees change colour and fall to the ground. Next spring, the trees will grow new leaves. Meanwhile, the piles of fallen leaves start to rot away. Millions of tiny worms and beetles live here. They chew up the leaves and help to mix them with the soil.

woodpecker

sapsucker

raccoon

earwig

earthworm

millipede

ground beetle

blue jay

opossum

warbler

white-tailed deer

skunk

A butterfly grows up

A butterfly starts life as an egg. After a few days, the egg hatches. A tiny caterpillar crawls out. The caterpillar feeds on leaves. It grows bigger and bigger. When it is big enough, the caterpillar grows a brown shell, called a pupa. Inside the pupa, the caterpillar changes. At last, the pupa splits open and out comes a butterfly!

purple hairsteak butterfly

eggs

pupa

caterpillar

▽ Black bears spend most of winter fast asleep. They curl up in a snug cave or hidden hollow. While they sleep, their bodies use less energy. This helps them to live through the cold months, when there is little food.

Stinky skunk

The skunk is one of the smelliest animals in the world. If it is attacked, it turns round and squirts a horrible, stinky liquid from near its bottom!

Wildlife in the rainforest

Imagine you are standing in the middle of a rainforest in South America. All around you, huge trees tower up towards the sky. At the very top, the trees end in a mass of leaves. Beneath the leaves it is dark and very hot. It rains here almost every day, so the air is damp. Because the rainforest is hot and wet, it is an ideal place for plants. Huge numbers of vines, ferns and flowers cover the trees. Insects, birds and climbing animals live up among the leaves. In fact, rainforests are home to more plants and animals than any other place in the world.

harpy eagle

Life on high

You will not see many animals on the ground. Most of them live high up in the tree tops. This is called the canopy. Up here, there is plenty of food. The rainforest is always warm, so the trees grow new leaves, fruits and seeds throughout the year.

▽ The arrow-poison frog grows up in a pond up a tree! The mother frog carries her tadpoles on her back through the leaves until she sees a plant called a bromeliad. Its cup-shaped leaves catch rainwater. The frog puts her tadpoles into the water, where they can grow up in their own private pool.

▽ The spider monkey swings through the branches. It uses its tail as well as its arms and legs.

▽ The macaw cracks nuts with its tough bill.

▽ The sloth hangs upside down from a branch, and moves very slowly.

▽ The tiny hummingbird sips nectar from flowers through its long bill.

A cat that can fish!

The jaguar loves to eat fish. It catches them just like a fisherman. The jaguar puts the tip of its tail in the water. Fish swim up to look at the twitching tail – and in a flash the jaguar turns and grabs them!

buttress roots

potto

▽ Some rainforest animals are very hard to spot, because their shape and colour make them look like something else. Leaf insects are green, and their bodies look just like leaves. This helps them to hide from their enemies.

Tree supports

Some rainforest trees are as tall as an apartment block. But their roots do not go down very deep, and so do not support the tree well. If the top of a tree is very heavy, it may fall over in a storm. Some kinds of tree have roots called buttresses. These stick out from the trunk and prop it up.

19

Wildlife in the desert

The Sahara in Africa is the biggest desert in the world. It is as big as the USA! Most of the Sahara is bare and dry, with scattered rocks, gravel or plain sand. It hardly ever rains. During the day it is very hot, but at night it quickly cools down. Animals and plants have to live with little water, and they must survive the fierce heat of the sun.

Keeping cool

Very few animals move about during the day. The heat of the sun would dry out their bodies. Mammals, such as the fennec fox and the gerbil, hide under rocks and in burrows. In these shady places it is much cooler. As soon as the sun goes down, the animals come out to hunt for food.

▽ The fennec fox uses its huge ears to keep cool. The thin ear flaps contain many tiny blood vessels close to the surface. As blood moves through these vessels, the fox loses its warmth to the outside air.

sand grouse

▷ The sand grouse has to fly a long way to find water. But its young cannot fly. How do they get a drink? The adult sand grouse has spongy feathers on its front. It soaks these feathers in water, then flies home. The young suck the water from the feathers.

cactus

▷ Sand is hard to walk on, and during the day it becomes scorching hot. But desert creatures still find ways to move about. The sidewinder snake moves along sideways. Only a small part of its body touches the sand at a time. The skink swims through the sand by wriggling its body.

sidewinder

esparto grass

△ Plants need water to live and grow. But in the desert there is hardly any moisture. So desert plants have special ways of keeping water. Some store it in their stems or roots. The leaves of esparto grass curl up so that they are shaded from the sun.

skink

! What a thirst!

The camel can walk for several days in the desert without drinking at all. But at the end of that time, it will drink as much as 180 litres of water – that is the same as 540 cans of drink!

21

Wildlife in Arctic lands

Winter is very long in the Arctic lands called tundra.
For nine months the ground is frozen, and covered in ice
and snow. During most of that time, there is no sun at all.
But in March the sun appears at last and the short summer
begins. The heat melts the surface of the frozen ground,
forming pools and bogs. Over the next few weeks, plants
flower, insects lay eggs and animals hurry to mate and
find food. Soon winter will be here again.

Arctic tern

caribou

Summer visitors

Many animals come to the
tundra just for the summer, when
there is plenty of food. Caribou arrive in huge
herds to feed on leaves and tiny plants called
lichens. Birds come to eat the mosquitoes and
other insects which hatch in the boggy pools.
But the Arctic tern travels furthest of all. It
rears its young near the North Pole, then flies
right across the world to Antarctica for the
southern summer.

Arctic fox

△ The Arctic willow is one
of the few trees on the
tundra. It does not grow
upwards, but sideways.
This keeps it close to the
ground, sheltered from
the icy winds.

◁ In winter, the Arctic fox grows a special new coat. It is thick, to keep out the cold, and white, so that the fox is difficult to see against the snow. In summer, its coat turns brown again. Other animals, such as the Arctic hare and the ptarmigan, also have white winter coats.

◁ Musk oxen can move quickly, but they do not run away from packs of hunting wolves. Instead, the oxen stand in a circle with their long curved horns facing outwards. Their young shelter in the centre of the circle, safe from the wolves.

▽ Lemmings spend the harsh winters safe in burrows under the snow. Here, they look for leaves, roots and stems to eat. In summer, when the snow melts, they dig burrows in the hard ground. But outside their burrows, they must beware of snowy owls and other fierce hunters.

23

Wildlife in the ocean

The waters of the South Pacific are warm and full of light. Many wonderful creatures live here – coloured fishes, sea urchins, giant squid, sea slugs and sharks. But the most wonderful of all are the corals. Corals are tiny animals, which build themselves houses of limestone. Over many years, their stone houses have built up into huge coral reefs.

▽ The squid looks clumsy, but can move very fast – it is jet-propelled! It fills itself up with water, then squirts the water out through a tube. This water "jet" sends the squid shooting along.

great white shark

jacks

squid

elkhorn coral

green turtle

sea fan

giant clam

sea cucumber

stonefish

stagshorn coral

Food for giants

The sea is full of tiny plants and animals – so tiny that you can hardly see them without a microscope. This mixture of creatures is called plankton. Plankton is a vital source of food for many other animals, from shrimps to jellyfish. The biggest eaters of plankton are whales. The blue whale is the largest animal in the world, but it lives on tiny plankton.

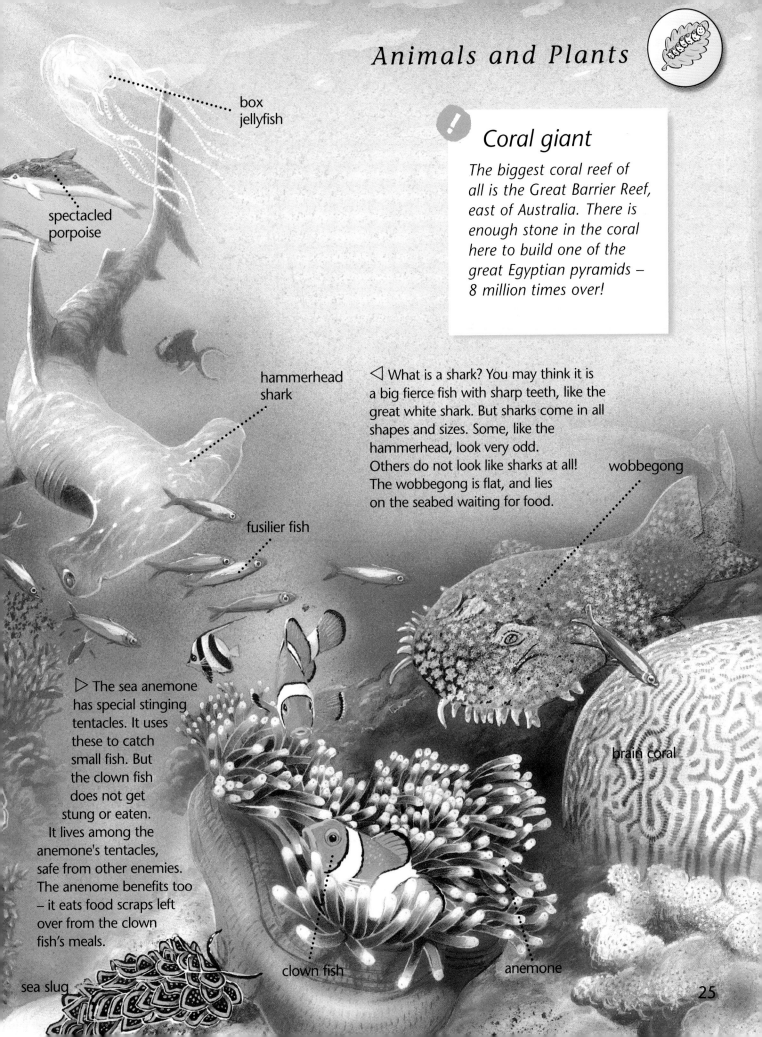

box
jellyfish

spectacled
porpoise

Coral giant

*The biggest coral reef of
all is the Great Barrier Reef,
east of Australia. There is
enough stone in the coral
here to build one of the
great Egyptian pyramids –
8 million times over!*

hammerhead
shark

◁ What is a shark? You may think it is
a big fierce fish with sharp teeth, like the
great white shark. But sharks come in all
shapes and sizes. Some, like the
hammerhead, look very odd.
Others do not look like sharks at all!
The wobbegong is flat, and lies
on the seabed waiting for food.

wobbegong

fusilier fish

▷ The sea anemone
has special stinging
tentacles. It uses
these to catch
small fish. But
the clown fish
does not get
stung or eaten.
It lives among the
anemone's tentacles,
safe from other enemies.
The anenome benefits too
– it eats food scraps left
over from the clown
fish's meals.

brain coral

sea slug

clown fish

anemone

Animals in danger

Have you ever seen a dodo? Or a quagga? It is not likely because these animals are extinct. This means that every one of them has died – there are none left in the world. Thousands of different animal and plant species have become extinct. Many disappeared quite naturally long ago. Others are in danger today, because people hunt them, or because we are changing the places where these animals and plants live.

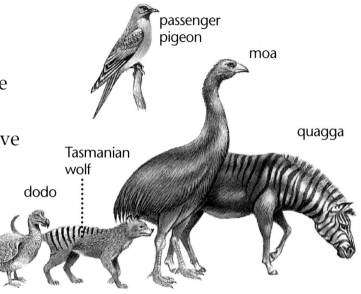

passenger pigeon

moa

quagga

Tasmanian wolf

dodo

△ All of these animals have died out – mainly because of what people have done. Hunters have killed some of them. Farmers, loggers and builders have taken away the homes and food supplies of others.

▽ These are just a few of the many animals that are in danger of extinction today.

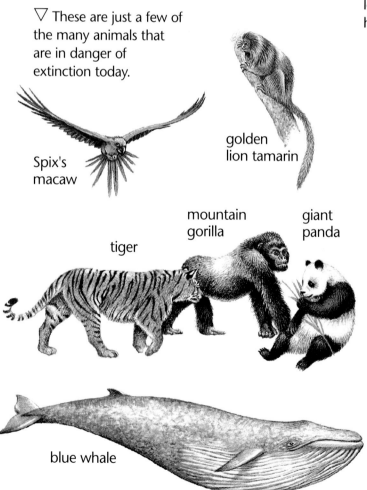

Spix's macaw

golden lion tamarin

mountain gorilla

giant panda

tiger

blue whale

What you can do

WWF

In some places, things are slowly changing for the better. Many animals are now protected, and there are special reserves where they can live safely. You can help to look after wildlife, too. In your local area there are probably groups that help to save endangered species. You could join one of these groups, or get in touch with the World Wide Fund For Nature, which helps wildlife all over the world. Its address is Panda House, Weyside Park, Godalming, Surrey, GU7 1XR.

Glossary

amphibian an animal such as a frog or toad, that lives in the water when it is young, but breathes air when it grows up.

arthropod a group of animals that includes insects, spiders and crabs.

bacteria very simple creatures made of a single cell. Some bacteria cause disease.

bog an area of wet, spongy ground.

carbon dioxide a gas in the air. When we breathe out, we get rid of unwanted carbon dioxide from our bodies.

cell tiny parts from which all living things are made.

coral tiny animals that live in groups and have stony skeletons. When the animals die, their skeletons form a kind of colourful rock.

desert an area where hardly any rain falls. Few plants and animals can live there because it is so dry.

fern a plant with feathery leaves and no flowers.

fossil the remains of a plant or animal from long ago. Many fossils are found inside rocks.

fungus a kind of plant that cannot make food using air and sunlight. Mushrooms are one type of fungus.

gazelle an animal like a deer, found in Africa and Asia.

gills the "lungs" of water-living animals, which allow them to breathe.

grub a fat, worm-like creature. The young of insects are grubs.

horsetail a type of water plant with a jointed stem and thin, green branches that look like the hairs of a horse's tail.

mammal any kind of animal where the mother feeds her babies with her own milk. People, seals, whales and most furry animals are mammals.

mollusc an animal with a soft body and a protective shell. Snails, shellfish and squids are all molluscs.

moss a simple kind of plant that does not have flowers and grows in damp places.

nectar a sweet liquid made by flowers.

rainforest a thick tropical forest, where a lot of rain falls all year round.

reptile a goup of animals that includes snakes, crocodiles, lizards and tortoises.

sea urchin a round, spiny animal that lives in the sea.

South Pacific the southern part of the Pacific Ocean.

tadpole a young frog or toad, which can only live in water.

termite an insect like an ant, which lives in large colonies.

vine a climbing or trailing plant.

Index

Acknowledgements

Abbreviations: t = top; b = bottom; c = centre; l = left; r = right; (back) = background; (fore) = foreground.

Illustrations

Cover John Butler; back cover t Terry Riley; back cover b Brinn Edwards; 5 Michael Strand; 6l John Davies; 6r Linden Artists; 7cl, c Peter Visscher; 7cr Tim Halliday; 7bl Scot Ritchie; 8–9 (fore) Peter Visscher; 8–9 (back) Julian Baker; 10 (fore) Terry Riley; 10 (back) Nick Hawken; 11cr Terry Riley; 11bl Scot Ritchie; 12–13 by John Davies; 13br Scot Ritchie; 14–15 Sean Milne; 16–17 John Butler; 17br Scot Ritchie; 18–19 Steve Roberts; 19tr Scot Ritchie; 20–23 John Butler; 24–25 Brinn Edwards; 26 Steve Roberts.

Photographs

The publishers would like to thank the following for permission to reproduce photographs:

77t Natural History Photo Archive (NHPA); 81 Corbis; 83tr Planet Earth Pictures; 91bl; 95t Natural History Photo Archive (NHPA); 96b Natural History Photo Archive (NHPA); 26cr World Wide Fund for Nature (WWF).